Original title:
The Gift of Love

Copyright © 2024 Swan Charm
All rights reserved.

Author: Kaido Väinamäe
ISBN HARDBACK: 978-9916-89-097-4
ISBN PAPERBACK: 978-9916-89-098-1
ISBN EBOOK: 978-9916-89-099-8

Tender Gestures

A gentle touch, a soft embrace,
In quiet moments, love finds its place.
A sweet smile shared, a knowing glance,
Tender gestures weave a timeless dance.

Each whispered word, a soothing balm,
In storms of life, they can keep us calm.
With hands entwined, we face the night,
Tender gestures bring warmth and light.

Fireside Stories

Crackling flames, a warm retreat,
Gathered close, where hearts can meet.
Tales of old, in shadows cast,
Fireside stories, memories vast.

Laughter rings, as night unfolds,
In golden glows, our lives are told.
With every tale, our spirits soar,
Fireside stories, forevermore.

Raindrops of Joy

Pattering softly on the ground,
Raindrops of joy, a soothing sound.
Each droplet dances, free and bright,
A symphony of pure delight.

They kiss the earth, a gentle plea,
Refreshing life, wild and free.
In every splash, a secret shown,
Raindrops of joy, we call our own.

Heartfelt Moments

In fleeting time, we find our way,
Heartfelt moments, here to stay.
A laugh, a tear, a shared gaze,
Each cherished second, life's sweet praise.

In quiet space, where love resides,
Heartfelt moments, where joy abides.
A simple touch, a shared sigh,
Heartfelt moments that amplify.

Balloons in the Sky

Bright balloons drift high,
Floating in the blue,
Whispers of a dream,
Carried on the view.

Colors dance and sway,
Joy within the air,
Children's laughter sings,
With a sweet affair.

Clouds become their play,
Chasing every wish,
Up above the trees,
An unspoken bliss.

As the sun does set,
Shadows start to blend,
Balloons wave goodbye,
On the breeze they send.

Crimson Threads

In the autumn breeze,
Leaves like fire fall,
Crimson threads below,
Nature's vibrant call.

Whispers through the trees,
Tales of days gone by,
Woven in the gold,
Underneath the sky.

Each step holds a tale,
Stories from the ground,
Crimson threads unite,
In silence profound.

Time begins to fade,
Yet the colors stay,
A tapestry bright,
At the close of day.

The Taste of Sweetness

Honey on my lips,
Fruits in summer's glow,
Every bite a joy,
Moments that we know.

Soft and gentle touch,
Savoring the day,
Sunshine in each drop,
Drifting far away.

Sugar in the air,
Laughter on the breeze,
Echoes of delight,
Bringing hearts to ease.

Joy in every taste,
Memories in bloom,
Tenderness like rain,
Filling up the room.

Letters in the Clouds

Words drift high above,
Written in the sky,
Messages of love,
As the day goes by.

Puffy letters swirl,
Carried by the breeze,
Whispers soft and sweet,
Floating with such ease.

Each cloud holds a dream,
Stories to unfold,
Wishes painted white,
Against skies of gold.

We look up and smile,
Finding hope in words,
Letters in the clouds,
Sing like gentle birds.

Reflections of Trust

In whispers soft, the truth will shine,
A bond so strong, the stars align.
Through trials faced, we stand as one,
In shadows deep, our hearts have won.

Each secret shared, a gentle thread,
A tapestry of words unsaid.
With open hearts, we brave the night,
In faith we find our guiding light.

Together we rise, no fear, no doubt,
In harmony, we dance about.
Through storms and calm, we'll find our way,
In trust we grow, come what may.

Harvest of Kindness

In gentle hands, the seeds are sown,
The fruits of grace have brightly grown.
With every smile, a heart is healed,
In the warmth of hope, love is revealed.

Through each small act, a ripple spreads,
In kindness shared, our spirit treads.
Upon this earth, we sow and reap,
In every promise, our dreams we keep.

Together we gather, a vibrant hue,
In fields of mercy, we create anew.
With open hearts, we share our days,
In the harvest of kindness, love stays.

Journey of the Heart

Each step we take, a path unknown,
In whispers soft, our hearts have grown.
Through valleys deep, and mountains high,
With courage vast, we learn to fly.

In every tear, a lesson found,
In laughter's light, love knows no bound.
With every turn, a story unfolds,
In the journey of hearts, our truth is told.

Together we wander, hand in hand,
In this wondrous life, we understand.
Through every storm, we hold each other,
In the journey of the heart, we discover.

Embers of Intimacy

In silent nights, our souls entwine,
In every glance, our hearts align.
With gentle touch, the fire ignites,
In the dance of love, we reach new heights.

With whispered dreams, our spirits soar,
In every moment, we crave for more.
Through shadows cast, our trust remains,
In the embers of intimacy, love reigns.

Together we dwell, in sacred space,
In the warmth of closeness, we find our place.
With open hearts, we share our fears,
In the embers of love, we dry our tears.

Lanterns of Belonging

In the dusk's warm glow, we gather near,
Holding memories, laughter, and cheer.
Lanterns flicker, casting soft light,
Binding our hearts through the night.

Stories are woven with each gentle breeze,
Ancient whispers carried through trees.
Embers of friendship ignite the sky,
In this circle, we let worries fly.

Together we dance, our spirits align,
Holding hands, through the shadow we shine.
Under the stars, our dreams take flight,
Lanterns of belonging, our guiding light.

Shadows of Serenity

Beneath the branches, silence thrives,
In nature's embrace, our peace derives.
Gentle ripples on a serene lake,
Whispers of stillness, our hearts awake.

Shadows play softly on the ground,
In this sacred space, solace found.
A moment of truth, a breath so deep,
In the arms of serenity, we gently sleep.

Clouds drift slowly, painting the skies,
In the twilight glow, our spirits rise.
With every sigh, the world grows small,
Shadows of serenity, embracing us all.

The Alchemy of Us

In the cauldron of life, we blend and weave,
Moments of joy, in which we believe.
Alchemy stirs, transforming the day,
With every heartbeat, we find our way.

Golden laughter, like sunlit beams,
Crafting a world forged from dreams.
Glimmers of hope in difficult times,
The alchemy of us, in rhythm and rhymes.

Together we create, with passion divine,
A tapestry woven, a love that will shine.
In each other's arms, magic is found,
The alchemy of us, forever unbound.

Waves of Understanding

Upon the shore, the ocean roars,
With every wave, wisdom pours.
Ripples of thoughts, shared and kind,
Waves of understanding, gentle and blind.

In depths we dive, our fears we face,
Finding solace in this sacred space.
Tides of compassion, ebbing away,
Guiding our hearts as we learn to sway.

Every crest and trough, a lesson unfolds,
In the sea of connection, we are consoled.
With open hearts, we anchor and trust,
Riding the waves of understanding, we must.

Sailing on Gentle Currents

We drift on dreams, the sails are high,
Beneath the azure of the vast sky.
Waves whisper softly, a tender tune,
Guiding our hearts as we chase the moon.

The sun dips low, painting gold in its wake,
We dance with shadows, the night starts to break.
Stars twinkle bright, our compass in hand,
Together we wander, a voyage so grand.

The sea tells tales of love and of loss,
We navigate shores, embracing the gloss.
With each gentle push from the tide's embrace,
We find in each moment, a sacred place.

Together we laugh, we sing, we roam,
In every wave, we carve out our home.
With sails unfurled, we chase after dreams,
Sailing on currents, life's flowing streams.

Echoes of Laughter

In corners of rooms, the laughter takes flight,
Whispers of joy dance in the night.
Memories cherished, like fireflies gleam,
Filling our hearts with a marvelous dream.

Around the old table, tales intertwine,
The warmth of our bonds, forever a sign.
Each chuckle and grin, a thread finely spun,
Echoes of laughter, two hearts yet as one.

Through seasons of change, laughter remains,
A balm for the soul, softening pains.
In silent moments, it softly resides,
A melody lingering, where love abides.

Underneath starlight, we share our delight,
With echoes of laughter, we dance in the night.
Building a legacy, timeless and true,
Each giggle a treasure, binding me and you.

Pathways of Compassion

In the quiet places, our hearts start to meet,
With hands reaching out, we share every beat.
Together we walk on this fragile earth,
Finding our purpose, discovering worth.

With each gentle step, we learn to embrace,
The stories of others, each unique trace.
Compassion flows through, like a river so wide,
Uniting our souls, where love can reside.

Through valleys of sorrow and mountains of joy,
We gather the pieces like a well-loved toy.
Showing up for each other, we lift and we heal,
In pathways of compassion, our hearts truly feel.

In the tapestry woven with kindness and care,
We find our connection, a bond that we share.
With every kind gesture, a ripple goes forth,
Creating a world that knows love's true worth.

Canvas of Memories

On the canvas of time, we splash all our hues,
Strokes of affection and shadows of blues.
Each moment a color, each laugh a bright flare,
Painting our lives with beauty to share.

The palette of moments, both bitter and sweet,
Layers of lessons beneath our feet.
With every heartbeat, a brush in our hand,
Creating the portraits of a life well-planned.

From sunrise glimmers to twilight's soft sighs,
We cherish each moment that slowly flies.
In galleries hidden, our stories await,
Timeless reminders of love, never late.

We gather each memory, old treasures preserved,
Framing our journeys, the paths we deserve.
With colors of laughter, our hearts will display,
The canvas of memories, we paint every day.

Heartbeat of the Universe

In the silence, stars unfold,
Whispers of stories yet untold.
Galaxies dance in cosmic grace,
Timeless echoes, a sacred space.

From the depths, a pulse ignites,
A symphony of endless nights.
Planets spin in a swirling tune,
Together, they hum beneath the moon.

Light years cross in love's embrace,
Gravity's pull, a warm trace.
In every beat, a dream resides,
Cosmic love forever guides.

Nebulas paint the skies above,
In hues that whisper of pure love.
Each heartbeat wraps the vast unknown,
In unity, we are never alone.

Through the cosmic winds we soar,
The universe calls and we explore.
In every star, a heartbeat sings,
An endless tale of wondrous things.

Vows of Forever

With every sunrise, a promise dawns,
In whispered vows, our love adorns.
Through storms and sun, we stand so strong,
In a world where we both belong.

Hand in hand, we face the night,
Guided by love's eternal light.
Each heartbeat echoes, a sacred tune,
Binding our souls like the sun and moon.

In laughter's ring, our joy expands,
In quiet moments, fate's soft hands.
Together we weave a timeless thread,
In love's embrace, our fears are shed.

Through trials faced, we pledge our hearts,
In every challenge, love imparts.
With open arms, our spirits soar,
In this journey, forevermore.

In every glance, our future gleams,
In every dream, us, it seems.
Two souls entwined, a passionate fire,
In vows of forever, we never tire.

A Garden of Compassion

In the heart blooms a tender space,
Where kindness thrives in warm embrace.
Each petal soft, each color bright,
A garden nurtured in the light.

Seeds of hope in the soil are sown,
Watered by love, they've gently grown.
Compassion whispers, its voice so clear,
In every leaf, the world draws near.

In this haven, we find our peace,
Where worries melt, and hearts release.
The fragrance sweet, a balm for souls,
In this garden, the spirit strolls.

Through storms and winds, we stand as one,
Resilient roots, we've just begun.
For in our hearts, this truth will swell,
In a garden of compassion, all is well.

Together we bloom, in harmony,
Each flower a part of the story.
With every breath, this love expands,
In a world where hope forever stands.

Harmony of Hearts

In twilight's glow, our spirits meet,
A melody in the heart's own beat.
With every glance, a silent song,
In harmony, we both belong.

Through whispered dreams, our souls entwine,
In perfect rhythm, so divine.
Each moment shared, a sweet refrain,
In love's embrace, we feel no pain.

Like rivers flow towards the sea,
Our hearts unite, wild and free.
In laughter's echo, joy we find,
In every note, our hearts aligned.

With every challenge, we grow strong,
Two voices rise, a steadfast song.
In shadows cast, we'll never part,
For love's true path, guides every heart.

In the silence, let love arise,
A symphony beneath the skies.
Together we breathe, forever stirred,
In harmony of hearts, love's sweet word.

Harmony of Souls

In whispers soft, our voices blend,
A melody that knows no end.
With every laugh, with every sigh,
Together we soar, reaching the sky.

In silent glances, truth unfolds,
A bond so deep, it never grows old.
Our hearts entwined, like vines do climb,
In the dance of life, we find our rhyme.

Through stormy nights and sunny days,
We share the light in countless ways.
In every heartbeat, every tune,
We paint our love beneath the moon.

With hands held tight, we walk this road,
Together we lighten each heavy load.
In sacred space, we are embraced,
In the harmony, our souls are graced.

Canvas of Devotion

With every brush, a tale unfolds,
In vibrant hues, our love it molds.
On canvas wide, our dreams take flight,
In strokes of passion, pure delight.

Each color speaks of moments shared,
In whispers soft, how much we cared.
The lines we draw, both bold and fine,
In every stroke, your heart is mine.

From darkest shades to bright and clear,
We paint our hopes, we cast our fears.
In every layer, depths we find,
A masterpiece of heart and mind.

Through art we grow, through art we learn,
In every twist, our passions burn.
A canvas rich with memories bright,
In this devotion, our souls ignite.

Now and Always

In this moment, time stands still,
With every heartbeat, I feel the thrill.
Now and always, our love will grow,
In the gentle breeze, our destiny flows.

Each tick of clock, a promise made,
In shadows long, our dreams cascade.
Through every trial, every grace,
In your embrace, I find my place.

With every sunrise, a brand new start,
A symphony sung by two hearts.
Now and always, hand in hand,
In this beautiful journey, together we stand.

No mountain too high, no river too wide,
In every storm, I'll be your guide.
In laughter and tears, we'll find our way,
Now and always, come what may.

Unseen Connections

In quiet moments, eyes will meet,
A spark ignites, profound and sweet.
Unseen connections, subtle and rare,
In every glance, a whispered prayer.

Like threads of gold woven through time,
In silent spaces, our souls align.
In every heartbeat, a secret shared,
A bond unbroken, deeply cared.

With every step, our paths converge,
In hidden realms, our hearts emerge.
Through whispered winds, our spirits soar,
Unseen connections, forevermore.

In shadows cast, a light will shine,
In every moment, your hand in mine.
Together we rise, as stars unfold,
In unseen connections, a story told.

Wings of Serenity

In whispers soft, the breezes sway,
Where dreams take flight at break of day.
With open arms, the skies invite,
For peace resides in morning light.

The river flows, a gentle glide,
Reflecting hues, the world outside.
Each moment cherished, time stands still,
As hearts align with nature's will.

The mountains sigh, their shadows long,
They cradle hope in silent song.
With every step, the spirit soars,
In harmony with life's outdoors.

The clouds, like dreams, they drift and weave,
In patterns that we dare believe.
With every breath, the soul finds grace,
In tranquil skies, we find our place.

Blossoms of Trust

In gardens bright where petals bloom,
Their colors chase away the gloom.
With every scent, a tale unfolds,
Of trust that's forged in hearts, not gold.

Each bud that opens, tells a story,
Of loyalty that seeks no glory.
In friendship's shade, two souls align,
Their roots entangled, strong as vine.

Together thrive, through sun and rain,
In laughter shared, in moments plain.
The bond we weave, like vines in spring,
A tapestry of trust we bring.

From every leaf, each rustling sound,
A promise kept, where love is found.
In silence deep, we'll always stand,
With open hearts, we join our hands.

The Dance of Two

In twilight's shade, the stars ignite,
Two spirits swirl in soft moonlight.
With every step, their laughter sings,
A melody of countless things.

With hands entwined, they carve the night,
In perfect rhythm, pure delight.
The world around them fades away,
In fleeting moments, love will stay.

Each glance exchanged, a spark so bright,
In every twirl, a promise tight.
As whispers flow like gentle streams,
Their hearts reveal their truest dreams.

The dance goes on, no end in sight,
Two souls as one, beneath the light.
In every beat, their journey's shared,
In faith and love, they're truly paired.

Moonlit Promises

Under the glow, where shadows play,
Two hearts converge, come what may.
The night wraps love in silver thread,
As whispered words, sweet silence spread.

A promise made beneath the stars,
To chase away each fear, each scar.
The moonlight bathes their hopes in dreams,
In shared embraces, nothing's as it seems.

With every star, a wish is cast,
For moments held, they hold them fast.
Each heartbeat echoes love's refrain,
In tender nights, through joy and pain.

The dawn can wait, for now they sway,
In the stillness, night turns to day.
As memories bloom, no light can sever,
The promises made, we'll keep forever.

The Radiant Embrace

In the glow of morning light,
Two souls dance, eager and bright.
Every heartbeat sings a song,
Together, where they both belong.

With hands entwined, they tread the way,
Through fields of dreams, where they sway.
Whispers soft as summer rain,
In their silence, love's sweet gain.

Each moment wrapped in tender grace,
Finding solace in each embrace.
A tapestry of hopes we weave,
In the radiant light, they believe.

As shadows stretch and daylight fades,
With every step, their love cascades.
The warmth of passion, deep and true,
In their hearts, a world anew.

Underneath the twilight hue,
They share secrets, just a few.
In the heart's garden, blossoms bloom,
In their embrace, dispelling gloom.

Embrace of Hearts

Two wandering spirits, worlds apart,
Drawn together by a beat of heart.
In the warmth of love's embrace,
They find shelter, a sacred space.

With every laugh and every tear,
The melody of love draws near.
In every glance, a story told,
In the flame of warmth, they both hold.

From vibrant dawn to dusky night,
Their souls collide in pure delight.
Every whisper, every sigh,
Underneath the eternal sky.

The rhythm of their hearts a song,
In the dance of life, they belong.
With every stumble, every grace,
They embrace time, their sacred place.

Side by side as seasons change,
Their hearts entwined, a lovely range.
In this life, they find their part,
In the gentle, sweet embrace of hearts.

Whispers in the Breeze

A soft whisper through the trees,
Carried gently on the breeze.
Nature speaks in hushed tones clear,
A song of love that draws us near.

The rustling leaves, a sweet refrain,
Echo stories of joy and pain.
In every breath, we find release,
In whispers shared, we feel the peace.

As shadows dance with fleeting light,
Together, we'll chase the night.
In twilight's glow, secrets unfold,
Whispers of dreams, tender and bold.

The world around us fades away,
In this moment, come what may.
With hearts as one, we dare to stand,
In this tranquil, sacred land.

So let the breezes softly guide,
In every moment, be our pride.
For as long as the sun shall rise,
Whispers in the breeze shall be our ties.

Beneath Starlit Skies

Beneath the arch of sparkling night,
Two hearts collide in soft moonlight.
With every star, a wish is cast,
In their embrace, the world is vast.

The cool breeze carries their laughter,
In silence, dreams are what they're after.
Each twinkle holds a story bright,
Of love that shines like stars alight.

As constellations weave their tale,
Two hearts together shall not pale.
In the embrace of softest night,
They find their courage, pure delight.

Through cosmic waves, they drift and soar,
In this dance, they crave for more.
With every heartbeat, love expands,
Beneath the stars, their future stands.

In the end, when night must fade,
Together still, unafraid.
In every dawn, love will arise,
Forever danced beneath starlit skies.

Notes of Intimacy

In whispers soft, our secrets bind,
Two souls one melody, intertwined.
Fingers trace each silent thought,
In the quiet spaces love is sought.

Every glance ignites a spark,
In the stillness of the dark.
Hearts composed a gentle tune,
Underneath the silver moon.

Words unspoken, feelings clear,
In the space where souls appear.
A canvas rich with tender hues,
Where dreams unite, and love ensues.

Time suspends in sweet embrace,
Every moment holds its place.
In the symphony we play,
Intimacy guides our way.

Echoes of Embrace

In the arms of love, we find our peace,
Soft shadows wrap, worries cease.
With whispers low, secrets unfold,
In echoes of embrace, warmth takes hold.

The world outside fades, we stay still,
In this moment, our hearts fulfill.
With tender sighs that speak so loud,
In each other's gaze, we feel so proud.

Every heartbeat, a promise made,
In the silence, our fears fade.
In the closeness, we dare to believe,
That love's true power, we thus perceive.

In twilight's glow, together we dream,
Bathed in warmth, like a gentle stream.
Each moment shared, a treasure found,
In echoes of embrace, love is profound.

A Serenade for Two

Under the moon, we find our tune,
Soft whispers dance, hearts in bloom.
A melody plays, gentle and sweet,
In this moment, we feel complete.

Your hand in mine, a perfect fit,
In the silence, our souls commit.
A glance exchanged, a spark ignites,
In the serenade, love takes flight.

With every note, our dreams weave tight,
In twilight's glow, everything feels right.
Two hearts sync, in rhythm they move,
A symphony crafted, our love to prove.

In harmony's arms, we find our grace,
With laughter and joy, we fill our space.
As stars above begin to gleam,
In this serenade, we live our dream.

In the Glow of Kindness

In the quiet dusk, hearts align,
Gentle whispers, soft and divine.
A smile shared, like a bright sun,
Together we shine, two become one.

Acts of grace, small yet bright,
Lifting spirits, a warm light.
Kindness flows like a stream,
Binding us in a shared dream.

In laughter's echo, we find our way,
Heartfelt moments, here to stay.
With every gesture, love expands,
Creating bonds, uniting hands.

Through the struggles, we stand tall,
In the glow of kindness, we hear the call.
With open hearts, we embrace the night,
Together we rise, reaching new height.

Mosaics of Emotion

Each piece shines, a story told,
In the colors, bright and bold.
Fragments of laughter, tears, and sighs,
In this work, true love never lies.

Every shard, a moment's grace,
In the puzzle, find your place.
With each layer, we discover,
In the heart, no need to cover.

Together crafting tales of old,
In this artwork, our hands hold.
Textures rich with passion's light,
In the darkness, we create night.

With every piece, the beauty grows,
In the blend, our spirit flows.
Mosaics here, forever free,
In this tapestry, you and me.

Journey into Warmth

In the twilight, echoes call,
Two hearts rising, never fall.
With the dawn, a promise made,
In each breath, our love displayed.

On this path, the fire grows,
In the glow, each moment glows.
Gentle whispers fill the air,
In this warmth, we lay bare.

Every fear, a shadow fades,
In your arms, love cascades.
Together forging dreams anew,
In the light, just me and you.

Through the years, the seasons change,
Yet our hearts refuse to strange.
In this journey we embark,
Hand in hand, igniting spark.

Hand in Hand

Walking close, our shadows blend,
In this journey, you're my friend.
With each step, the world unfolds,
In your grip, the heart consoles.

Side by side, through thick and thin,
With your strength, I rise and win.
Every laugh, each tear we share,
Weaving bonds beyond compare.

Through the storm and bright sunlight,
Together, we will face the night.
In every trial, we will stand,
Finding comfort, hand in hand.

Paths may twist, but we'll remain,
Finding joy in every pain.
With every heartbeat, don't let go,
In this dance, our spirits flow.

Ripples of Joy

A ripple starts with a very small stone,
Spreading out wide, joy is sown.
With every laugh, a wave we create,
Together we float on shared fate.

In the dance of life, we swirl and spin,
Each joyful moment, a spark within.
From heart to heart, the energy flows,
In ripples of joy, our spirit grows.

Sunshine or rain, we cherish the ride,
With hands held tight, there's nothing to hide.
In shared adventures, we find our way,
Creating memories that forever stay.

Through ups and downs, we ride the tide,
In each other's laughter, we happily glide.
With every ripple, our hearts combine,
In the pool of joy, forever we shine.

The Language of Emotions

In whispers soft, feelings bloom,
A tender sigh can light the gloom.
Words unspoken, yet so clear,
In every glance, our hearts draw near.

Joy and sorrow intertwine,
With every beat, a new design.
Laughter dances on the air,
Silent tears, a burden shared.

The heart's dialect, rich and deep,
In every heartbeat, secrets keep.
A smile can heal, a frown can break,
In this language, all hearts awake.

Listen close, the tales they tell,
Of love's sweet rise, and painful swell.
In every moment, truth rings out,
Our spirits sing, there's never doubt.

Emotions swirl like painted skies,
Each stroke reveals the soul's true guise.
In this realm where hearts abide,
The language flows, a constant tide.

A Symphony of Hearts

In harmony, our voices rise,
A melody beneath the skies.
Each note a heartbeat, pure and true,
In symphony, I dance with you.

Strings and winds, a gentle blend,
Together, we begin to mend.
Soft percussion of tender touch,
In every note, I feel so much.

Chords of laughter, shades of pain,
A rhythm set by joy and rain.
Through crescendos, our spirits soar,
Together, we are evermore.

With every beat, a story spun,
A symphony of souls as one.
In silence, we find music's grace,
An endless waltz in time and space.

So let our hearts compose anew,
In vibrant hues, a world so true.
With each embrace, a sweet refrain,
A symphony that will remain.

Cherished Embraces

In arms wrapped tight, we find our peace,
A gentle hold, where worries cease.
Each heartbeat whispers, soft as air,
In cherished moments, love laid bare.

The warmth exchanged, a silent vow,
In every hug, we learn just how.
To cherish life, to keep it near,
In tender grips, we find the clear.

Beneath the stars, a sacred space,
In every smile, a soft embrace.
Memories cradled, hearts entwined,
In sweet reprieve, true joy we find.

Embraces caught like autumn leaves,
In every season, love believes.
The world may change, but we will stay,
In cherished arms, we'll find our way.

So hold me close, through night and day,
In every touch, let spirits play.
For in this bond, we are made whole,
Cherished embraces, one shared soul.

Harvest of Kindness

In fields of gold, we sow our seeds,
With hearts so pure, we tend to needs.
Every act, a gentle start,
In kindness, we share a part.

Seeds of love in soil will grow,
Beyond our reach, their impact flows.
A ripple sent, it circles round,
In acts of grace, our hopes are found.

Even small deeds light the way,
A smile can brighten someone's day.
In every gesture, we align,
The harvest swells, a grand design.

Together we create a stream,
Of kindness sown, a shared dream.
With open hearts, we light the dark,
In every soul, kindling a spark.

So gather close, let's plant the best,
In every heart, we'll find our rest.
The harvest waits, a gift so grand,
Through kindness, we will take our stand.

Serenade of the Heart

In whispers soft, the night takes flight,
A melody that stirs the soul's delight.
Stars above with shimmering grace,
Each twinkle a familiar face.

With every note, our spirits rise,
The song of love in tender skies.
Harmony flows through every beat,
Where two souls in rhythm meet.

A dance of hearts, a sweet embrace,
In every pause, we find our place.
The music lingers, sweet and clear,
Serenades we hold so dear.

In silence shared, a world we share,
A symphony beyond compare.
Together we weave, day by day,
The serenades that guide our way.

With fragrant dreams that softly start,
Our love, the serenade of heart.
In every moment, love's refrain,
A timeless song, forever plain.

Bridges of Understanding

In quiet moments, shadows fall,
We build the bridges, one and all.
With open hearts, we span the divide,
In every truth, we take great pride.

Through storms of doubt, our voices mesh,
Crafting connections, strong and fresh.
A reach of hands across the way,
Turning night into bright day.

In the tapestry of thoughts we share,
Threads of kindness woven with care.
Listening deep, we find the key,
Unlocking hearts, setting them free.

In laughter shared and tears embraced,
We find the paths we've bravely faced.
With every step, the world expands,
Creating bridges, hand in hands.

Together strong, through thick and thin,
Understanding blooms, where love begins.
In every word, a chance to see,
The bridges built, you and me.

Glimmers of Joy

In morning light, the world awakes,
With tales of joy, the heart remakes.
A dance of laughter, pure and bright,
Glimmers spark in soft daylight.

Through whispering winds, the children play,
Chasing dreams that twirl away.
Each giggle brightens every face,
Moments precious in their grace.

As blossoms bloom and colors gleam,
Life's simple gifts, we dare to dream.
In every hug and kindly glance,
Glimmers rise, inviting dance.

With friends beside, we share the fun,
Underneath the blazing sun.
Creating memories, warm and sweet,
In this carnival of heartbeat.

When shadows fall and nights grow long,
We hold the glimmers, ever strong.
In every dawn, new joys we find,
Glimmers that light our hearts and minds.

Seasons of Togetherness

In autumn's chill, we find the start,
Together we stand, heart to heart.
Leaves of gold dance through the air,
Each flutter whispers love and care.

Winter brings a cozy glow,
By the fire's warmth, our spirits grow.
With stories shared, and laughter bright,
We find our peace in the quiet night.

As springtime blooms, our hopes arise,
Painted skies and butterfly skies.
Hand in hand, through fragrant fields,
In every petal, joy reveals.

Summer's sun calls us outside,
With laughter flowing like the tide.
In every moment, we're alive,
Together we thrive, together we strive.

Through every season, we find our way,
In every challenge, come what may.
Together we stand, through thick and thin,
In the seasons of love, we begin again.

Whispers of Affection

In the quiet night, hearts conspire,
Glimmers of love spark like fire.
Through soft caress, our souls entwine,
In every whisper, your heart is mine.

Beneath the stars, secrets unfold,
Each tender word, a story told.
In gentle sighs, we breathe as one,
Two shadows dancing, softly spun.

The moon looks down, a watchful eye,
As dreams take flight, we learn to fly.
With every glance, a promise made,
In this realm of love, we won't evade.

Time stands still, the world does fade,
In the hush of night, we've serenade.
With each heartbeat, a vow renews,
In this embrace, there's nothing to lose.

So let the whispers linger and play,
In the dawn that breaks another day.
Forever forged, our hands entwined,
In the dance of love, forever blind.

Heartstrings Unraveled

Tangled threads of fate we weave,
In your gaze, I find reprieve.
With gentle hands, you pull me close,
In this moment, I need it most.

Each note we play, a symphony,
In every chord, you're all of me.
Fingers entwined, a silent pact,
In this harmony, there's no lack.

As seasons change and time flows free,
In your arms, I want to be.
With every smile, I come alive,
In your embrace, I truly thrive.

The world may spin, yet here we stay,
In the warmth of love, we find our way.
With laughter shared and moments bright,
You are my sun, my guiding light.

So let us dance through every storm,
In this love, we'll find our form.
With heartstrings taut and ever true,
Forever bound, just me and you.

Embrace in Bloom

In gardens lush, our love takes flight,
Petals unfold, a pure delight.
With every heartbeat, colors blend,
In this embrace, the world can mend.

The fragrant air, a whispered song,
In your warmth, I feel I belong.
Roots run deep, a bond so bright,
Together we bloom, a wondrous sight.

Sunrise brings the hope we need,
In your eyes, I plant a seed.
With gentle hands, we shape our fate,
In this dance, we illuminate.

Each moment cherished, time is ours,
Tomorrow's dreams, we'll reach the stars.
With every blush, love's fragrance spills,
In this embrace, our hopes fulfill.

Let petals fall, let seasons change,
In this garden, we'll never estrange.
With roots entwined, we'll stand so tall,
Forever embraced, we'll have it all.

Echoes of Tenderness

In the hush of night, whispers play,
Echoes of love, guiding our way.
Through shadows deep, your light breaks through,
In every heartbeat, I find you true.

Soft are the moments, held so dear,
In silent glances, no need for fear.
With every sigh, you touch my soul,
In the distance, you make me whole.

As stars alight, our dreams align,
In the gentle breeze, your hand is mine.
With every heartbeat, a story grows,
In this world of us, affection flows.

Let time forget, let stillness reign,
In this dance of love, we break the chain.
With whispers sweet, life's moments blend,
In echoes of tenderness, we transcend.

So here we stand, in twilight's glow,
In this embrace, love's fervor flows.
With every heartbeat, here we'll stay,
In the echoes of affection, our hearts play.

Lanterns of Connection

In darkness, lanterns glow bright,
They whisper warmth through the night.
Each flicker tells a tale,
Of bonds that never pale.

Hands entwined, stories shared,
In moments when we cared.
Threads of love weave our way,
Guiding hearts on the stray.

Under moonlit skies we meet,
In laughter, our souls greet.
With lanterns high, we'll dance,
Embracing life's own chance.

Through the storms, we will stand,
Connected, hand in hand.
In the quiet, feel the spark,
Our friendship lights the dark.

As candle flames flicker low,
In this bond, we will grow.
Together we'll light the way,
Each night turns into day.

A Tapestry of Souls

We weave our stories along the thread,
Each color a voice that's said.
In laughter and in strife,
A tapestry of life.

Stitches of joy and pain,
A design that's never plain.
In every loop and fold,
A memory to be told.

Threads of empathy intertwine,
Crafting bonds that brightly shine.
In the hands of fate, we trust,
A fabric rich and robust.

Each soul brings vibrant hue,
A legacy, born anew.
Together, we stand tall,
In unity, we shall not fall.

Through the time and space we share,
An artwork, bold and rare.
In the heart, a quiet role,
We are a tapestry of soul.

Echoes of Compassion

In the silence, hearts will speak,
Gentle whispers, strong, not weak.
Through the shadows of despair,
Compassion lingers in the air.

With open arms, we embrace,
Finding solace in this place.
Echoes of kindness flow,
Healing wounds, letting go.

Each voice a soothing balm,
In chaos, we find calm.
Through small acts, we ignite,
A spark that shines so bright.

Together, we rise and strive,
In unity, we feel alive.
A chorus of gentle grace,
Life's trials we will face.

The echoes ring, loud and clear,
A call to love, to draw near.
In our hearts, we plant the seeds,
Of compassion, born from needs.

Starlit Promises

Beneath the sky, stars align,
We whisper dreams, yours and mine.
In the silence, wishes take flight,
Starlit promises shine bright.

A galaxy of hopes we share,
In every glance, a tender care.
With each twinkle, a new start,
Mapping dreams in the heart.

Through the dark, we find our way,
Guided by the stars' ballet.
In constellations, stories unfold,
Of adventures yet untold.

Linked by the light from afar,
You and I, just like a star.
Together, we'll chase the dawn,
As shadows of night are drawn.

Underneath the endless skies,
In the stillness, our spirits rise.
With starlit promises as our guide,
In this journey, side by side.

Chasing Shadows Together

In the twilight's gentle glow,
We wander where wild rivers flow.
With laughter bright and spirits high,
We chase the shadows in the sky.

Footsteps echo on the ground,
Silent whispers all around.
Hand in hand, we'll find our place,
In the warmth of soft embrace.

As the stars begin to shine,
Your heart beats gently next to mine.
With every dream, we take a flight,
Chasing shadows through the night.

With hopes as bold as morning sun,
In every battle, we have won.
We'll paint the world in colors bright,
Chasing shadows, a pure delight.

Through the mist, we find our way,
In the dance of dusk and day.
With every step, our spirits soar,
Chasing shadows forevermore.

Woven Dreams

In a world of fabric fine,
We weave our hopes, your hand in mine.
Stitch by stitch, we craft a tale,
Of woven dreams that shall not pale.

Threads of gold and silver bright,
Play in the tapestry of night.
With every knot, our love's embraced,
In this design, our souls are traced.

Through vibrant colors, we embark,
Creating art that leaves a mark.
In the silence, stories bloom,
Woven dreams in every room.

As we unravel fears and doubt,
We'll find the strength to stand and shout.
Together in this vibrant seam,
We'll dance beneath the moonlit beam.

In every thread, a memory shines,
A bond that time cannot confine.
Together, always, we will appear,
In woven dreams, forever near.

Treasures of the Soul

Deep within, a spark ignites,
In whispered truths and starry nights.
Within our hearts, the treasures lie,
Waiting for wings, prepared to fly.

In the quiet of our gaze,
We'll uncover hidden ways.
Gemstones pure, in shadows found,
The treasures of the heart abound.

Through every storm, we will endure,
With faith and love, our souls are pure.
Like rivers that forever flow,
Treasures of the soul will grow.

With every step, we'll seek and find,
The essence that connects mankind.
In laughter and in whispered tears,
Treasures woven through the years.

So take my hand and journey near,
In every heartbeat, hold me dear.
Together, we will light the whole,
As we unveil the treasures of the soul.

A Dance of Two

In the moonlight's soft embrace,
We find our rhythm, find our space.
With every sway, our spirits tune,
In the magic of the evening's bloom.

As the stars begin to gleam,
We'll dance together, dream by dream.
With every step, our hearts align,
In the duet, your soul and mine.

Spinning softly, we glide and flow,
With every turn, love's flames do glow.
In this dance, we leave no trace,
But the joy of shared embrace.

We'll twirl beneath the endless sky,
In harmony, we'll always fly.
With hearts entwined, we'll find our tune,
In the rhythm of the silver moon.

So let the world around us fade,
In every note, our love displayed.
With every beat, our spirits woo,
In this timeless dance of two.

Tides of Affection

Waves crash softly on the shore,
Each whisper carries love once more.
In the moonlight, feelings glide,
Hearts entwined in the rising tide.

Glimmers dance as stars align,
Every moment, pure and fine.
With every ebb, our spirits swell,
In this tide, we find our shell.

Footprints traced in golden sand,
Hand in hand, we make our stand.
The ocean hums our secret tune,
Under the watchful eye of the moon.

Softly spoken, sweet caress,
In each wave, we find our bliss.
Flowing like the endless sea,
In your eyes, I long to be.

As the horizon stretches far,
You're my sun, my guiding star.
With each tide, our love will grow,
Forever in this ebb and flow.

A Mosaic of Memories

Fragments of laughter, colors bright,
Every moment feels just right.
In the gallery of our days,
Memories woven through sun's rays.

Each smile captured, every tear,
A tapestry that draws you near.
Time stands still as stories weave,
In our hearts, we choose to believe.

Photographs with edges worn,
In our minds, love is reborn.
Every glance, a tale retold,
Through the years, our bond unfolds.

From golden mornings to starry nights,
Together we embrace new heights.
Every chapter, every line,
In this mosaic, hearts entwine.

With each fragment, our canvas grows,
In the silence, our love flows.
A masterpiece made of sweet time,
In this journey, our hearts chime.

The Colors of Togetherness

In the palette of shared dreams,
Life's brush creates vibrant themes.
Shades of laughter, strokes of grace,
In every moment, love finds space.

Sunset hues of orange and red,
Wrap our hearts, a soft thread.
Through whispers shared and glances sweet,
In this dance, we find our beat.

From deep blues to gentle green,
Every color, a story seen.
With a touch, we blend and sway,
In this canvas, come what may.

Bright yellows of joy, light our way,
In every challenge, we choose to stay.
A masterpiece in the making,
With every love, we're celebrating.

Together we paint, forever bold,
In strokes of warmth, our love unfolds.
The colors blend, our hearts confess,
In this tapestry of togetherness.

Sunset Soiree

The horizon glows, a warm embrace,
As day fades softly, we find our place.
Beneath the sky of gold and pink,
In this moment, we pause and think.

Candles flicker in the gentle breeze,
A symphony of rustling leaves.
With laughter shared and stories spun,
In the fading light, we become one.

Cheers resound as glasses clink,
Under stars that glimmer and wink.
Each sunset whispers secrets true,
In twilight's hue, it's me and you.

As shadows stretch, our dreams ignite,
In the calm of approaching night.
Every heartbeat, a cherished sound,
In this soiree, love knows no bound.

With vibrant skies as our backdrop,
In each moment, let our joy swap.
Together we'll dance 'til night takes flight,
In the beauty of sunset's light.

Radiance of Companionship

In quiet corners, hearts align,
Laughter dances, souls entwined.
Through whispered secrets, dreams take flight,
Together shining, pure and bright.

With every moment, warmth we share,
A bond unbroken, beyond compare.
Through stormy days and skies of gray,
Your presence glows, lighting the way.

Through every trial, side by side,
With trust that stirs, we can't divide.
Sunlight filters through our days,
In every glance, love's gentle blaze.

The journey's sweet with you so near,
In silent laughter, love's sincere.
A canvas painted, memories flow,
In the gallery of life, our hearts glow.

Together we'll face the unknown tide,
In the heart's harbor, there's nowhere to hide.
United in spirit, hand in hand,
In the radiance of love, forever we stand.

Echoes of Tenderness

In gentle whispers, love awakens,
Soft as shadows, never forsaken.
With every beat, a silent song,
In tender echoes, we belong.

A secret language, eyes convey,
In fleeting moments, hearts obey.
Through silent tears, and softened sighs,
Our souls entwined, no need for lies.

The warmth of presence, close and dear,
In sweet surrender, we draw near.
Through softest nights and dawns anew,
Together weaving, love so true.

In every heartbeat, love resounds,
A melody found in simple sounds.
With every touch, a promise made,
In echoes of tenderness, love won't fade.

In the dance of shadows, we find grace,
In every moment, a warm embrace.
Through the quiet, our spirit soars,
In the heart's chamber, forever yours.

Sunshine of the Spirit

With morning light, our dreams arise,
A canvas brushed with vibrant skies.
In laughter's glow, we dance and play,
The sunshine of spirit brightens our way.

Through gentle breezes and golden rays,
Together we navigate life's maze.
In every heartbeat, joy takes flight,
A symphony woven in pure delight.

In sunset's glow, we pause and breathe,
With every moment, we both believe.
Through trials faced, we stand as one,
In the light of hope, our battles won.

In the warmth of love, shadows cease,
Together we find our sweet release.
With every sunrise, a brand-new start,
In sunshine's embrace, you hold my heart.

Through every storm, our spirits soar,
In unity found, we open the door.
With radiant laughter, we boldly live,
In the sunshine of spirit, love gives.

A Symphony of Emotions

In melodies sweet, our hearts compose,
A symphony where deep love flows.
With every note, our story's told,
In the dance of feelings, pure and bold.

Through highs and lows, we harmonize,
In crescendos bright, under vast skies.
With gentle whispers, each chord refined,
In the rhythm of souls, perfectly aligned.

Through piano's soft and violin's sighs,
In laughter's rise, love never dies.
In every heartbeat, a rhythm found,
In the symphony's pulse, our dreams resound.

With every chorus sung so clear,
In the art of love, we draw near.
Hand in hand, we dance the night,
In the symphony of emotions, we find light.

In the echoes of time, our song remains,
A testament to love's sweet gains.
Through life's grand stage, let's play the part,
In a symphony woven from the heart.

Whispers of Promise

In twilight's glow, the secrets weave,
Soft echoes dance, and hearts believe.
With every sigh, a hope takes flight,
Whispers of promise greet the night.

A gentle breeze through branches sways,
Tales of the future in subtle ways.
Moonbeams kiss the dreams we hold,
Carving paths in silver and gold.

The stars align, a cosmic sign,
In every moment, your hand in mine.
Together we'll chase what lies ahead,
On whispered vows, our spirits tread.

As shadows stretch and daylight wanes,
Love blooms bright, despite the pains.
In every heartbeat, a reason to stay,
Whispers of promise guide our way.

With every dawn, the light renews,
Painting the world in vibrant hues.
In gardens where our hopes entwine,
Whispers of promise, forever align.

A Tapestry of Connections

Threads of laughter, woven tight,
In the fabric of day and night.
Colors blending, stories shared,
A tapestry of love prepared.

With every stitch, a memory made,
In the warmth of bonds that never fade.
Connected hearts in harmony,
A dance of souls, wild and free.

Woven paths through twists and turns,
In the flames of friendship, passion burns.
Together we rise, facing the storm,
In the weave of life, we're safe and warm.

Each connection, a vibrant hue,
Painting our lives in shades of true.
Through joy and pain, we find our way,
A tapestry of connections on display.

As time unravels, still we hold,
The threads of stories yet untold.
In this art of being, we will find,
A tapestry of love, forever intertwined.

Blossoms in the Rain

Gentle drops on petals fall,
Nature's music, a soothing call.
Each blossom lifts its head with grace,
In the rain, they find their place.

Colors bloom in soft embrace,
Nourished deep, they find their space.
A dance of life in every tear,
Blossoms in the rain, bright and clear.

With every shower, they come alive,
In the tempest, they learn to thrive.
A reminder that storms must pass,
Blossoms in the rain, strong as glass.

Their fragrance whispers tales of hope,
In every storm, a chance to cope.
Through trials faced and battles won,
Blossoms in the rain, we rise as one.

In gardens lush, where raindrops play,
Life's symphony, come what may.
These lovely blooms, a sign so true,
Blossoms in the rain, me and you.

Moonlit Promises

Underneath the silver glow,
Secrets shared between us flow.
In the night, our dreams take flight,
Moonlit promises shine so bright.

Whispers soft like velvet skies,
In the shadows, truth never lies.
Hand in hand, we wander wide,
Moonlit promises as our guide.

Stars above, they watch and gleam,
In their light, we find our dream.
With every step, a story grows,
Moonlit promises, love bestows.

As silver beams on lovers shine,
In your heart, I know you'll find.
An endless bond that knows no end,
Moonlit promises, our hearts blend.

Through every season, night and day,
In moonlit magic, come what may.
Together, we'll forever stay,
Moonlit promises lead our way.

Threads of Devotion

In quiet whispers, hearts align,
A tapestry woven, thread by thread.
In moments cherished, love defined,
Each stitch a promise, softly said.

Hand in hand, we walk this road,
Barefoot on the path we tread.
Through storms and sun, our souls bestowed,
In threads of gold, softly spread.

The fabric of our dreams unfolds,
With colors rich, and stories spun.
In laughter's echo, warmth enfolds,
Together, we are never done.

Through trials faced, our bonds grow strong,
In shadows cast, we find our way.
With every heartbeat, love belongs,
A symphony that will not sway.

As time weaves on, and seasons change,
Our threads remain forever tight.
In devotion's dance, we rearrange,
A masterpiece in love's true light.

Radiance of Togetherness

In morning's glow, we rise as one,
The world awakens, full of grace.
With laughter bright, our hearts do run,
In every glance, a warm embrace.

Through sunlit paths, our spirits soar,
In every step, we find delight.
Together, stronger than before,
Under the stars, our dreams take flight.

In quiet moments, hands entwined,
We share our hopes, our fears laid bare.
A bond unbroken, hearts aligned,
In every heartbeat, love declares.

As twilight falls, the colors blend,
The sky ablaze, a canvas wide.
With you beside me, time will bend,
In radiant hues, we'll take our ride.

In every whisper, love's refrain,
We weave our stories, side by side.
In the soft glow, we'll always gain,
The beauty found in hearts allied.

Moments Cloaked in Warmth

Beneath the stars, we find our calm,
In cozy nights, where dreams begin.
With whispered words, like soothing balm,
We shed the world, let love win.

A crackling fire, shadows dance,
In every flicker, memories flow.
Wrapped in warmth, a sweet romance,
Together, lighter than the snow.

Through winter's chill, our spirits thrive,
In laughter shared, the cold retreats.
In every heartbeat, we survive,
Moments cherished, life completes.

The world outside fades far away,
As time stands still, we hold it tight.
In every breath, love finds its way,
Cloaked in warmth, our hearts ignite.

At dawn's first blush, a new embrace,
In golden light, we start anew.
With every moment, find our place,
In warmth, forever me and you.

Serendipity's Caress

In chance encounters, fate aligns,
With every glance, a spark ignites.
A dance of hearts, in pure designs,
Serendipity's soft delights.

Through tangled paths, we wander free,
In twilit dreams, our secrets shared.
With every step, you're here with me,
A universe that shows it cared.

In hidden corners, stories bloom,
With laughter bright, we cast our nets.
Embracing all, dispelling gloom,
In serendipity, no regrets.

The magic lies in moments spun,
In whispered dreams, our spirits fly.
Together basking in the sun,
In soft caresses, you and I.

As seasons change, and time runs wild,
We'll treasure all that life bestows.
With open hearts, like curious child,
In serendipity, love grows.

Cascades of Memories

Whispers of laughter fill the air,
Echoes of joy beyond compare.
Images dance like sunlight's gleam,
Carving our hearts in a timeless dream.

Faded photographs, a bittersweet trace,
Every moment a cherished embrace.
The river flows with stories untold,
In cascades of warmth, we find our gold.

Memories shimmer like stars above,
Each glimmer a reminder of love.
The past wraps around in a sweet refrain,
Lingering softly like a gentle rain.

Through valleys of time, we wander still,
In search of the echoes our hearts fulfill.
Every heartbeat a step we take,
In the flow of time, we awake.

So here we stand, hand in hand,
In the music of memories, we understand.
The beauty of life in each tender sigh,
As cascades of memories whisper goodbye.

Gifts Wrapped in Time

Life's treasures hide in moments rare,
Wrapped with love and tender care.
Each day unfolds a brand new gift,
In simple smiles, our spirits lift.

A quiet word, a knowing glance,
In these gestures, we find our chance.
To unwrap the layers, soft and light,
Revealing joys that ignite the night.

Time is a ribbon, woven with grace,
Tying together our sacred space.
In laughter's echoes, we softly bind,
The gifts of the heart, intertwined.

As seasons change, new presents arise,
Wrapped in the warmth of summer skies.
Each moment a treasure, bright and bold,
In memory's embrace, we gently hold.

So cherish the moments, both big and small,
For each is a gift that answers our call.
In every heartbeat, in every rhyme,
Lie the gifts of our lives, wrapped in time.

Footsteps in the Sand

On golden shores, our footprints lay,
Marking moments of a sunlit day.
Waves kiss the land, a gentle embrace,
In each tiny step, we find our place.

The tide pulls back, yet memories stay,
In grains of sand that softly sway.
With every rush, the ocean speaks,
Of dreams and hopes that time still seeks.

Together we walk, hand in hand,
Tracing stories written in sand.
Each laugh, each sigh, a breath of time,
Carved in nature's rhythm and rhyme.

As dusk descends, the colors blend,
Every wave a letter we send.
To the shores of tomorrow, we will stride,
With footprints united, side by side.

So let us dance as the moonlight glows,
In the sands of time, where love still flows.
For every step speaks volumes anew,
In the whispers of waves, I find you.

In this fleeting world, our marks will last,
Footsteps in the sand, bound to the past.
Yet present and future blend in the sea,
Creating a journey, just you and me.

Beneath the Cherry Blossoms

Petals drift down like whispered dreams,
Beneath the boughs, the sunlight beams.
A dance of pink in the gentle breeze,
Awakens the heart like the sweetest tease.

Laughter rings out, as couples stroll,
In the enchanting scene, we lose control.
Each blossom a promise of love to ignite,
A canvas of beauty, pure and bright.

With every step, the petals fall,
A carpet of wishes, enchanting us all.
As shadows grow long in the afternoon light,
We find our peace in this floral delight.

Time pauses here, in this sacred space,
As nature wraps us in her embrace.
Beneath the cherry blossoms, we bloom,
In a world painted bright, dispelling all gloom.

So let's hold this moment, forever and true,
Under the blossoms where dreams come through.
In a flurry of petals, our hearts shall soar,
Beneath the cherry blossoms, we seek evermore.

Threads of Affection

In the quiet whispers of the night,
Our hearts entwined, they take flight.
With every glance, a story's spun,
Threads connecting, two become one.

Gentle laughter, soft as the breeze,
Moments cherished, hearts at ease.
In the tapestry of time, we weave,
A bond so strong, we dare believe.

Through trials faced, together we stand,
Hand in hand, we craft our land.
In the warmth of love, we'll find our way,
Guiding each other, come what may.

Every touch, a promise made,
In our haven, fears will fade.
With vibrant hues, our dreams take form,
In the garden of love, we're reborn.

As seasons change, our roots run deep,
In the embrace of love, we leap.
Bound by the threads that never fray,
Together we'll dance, come what may.

Moments of Togetherness

In the gentle hush of morning light,
We find our joy, our hopes in sight.
Coffee brewed, laughter fills the air,
These moments precious, beyond compare.

As twilight falls, we stroll along,
Hand in hand, a sweet love song.
With every step, a memory blooms,
In quiet spaces, love's warmth looms.

Sharing secrets beneath starlit skies,
In your gaze, the world complies.
With whispers soft, we tell our tales,
In the night air, our laughter sails.

Together we craft well-worn paths,
In the dance of life, we find our laughs.
With open hearts, we embrace the day,
In every moment, love finds a way.

Through life's journey, side by side,
In every challenge, we'll confide.
Together forever, our spirits bind,
In these moments, peace we find.

Eternal Flame

In the depths of night, a spark ignites,
An eternal flame, love's guiding lights.
Through shadows cast, it brightly glows,
A beacon strong, where true love flows.

With every heartbeat, the fire grows,
Two souls intertwined, the warmth bestows.
Through storms and trials, we hold it dear,
In the silence, your heart I hear.

The dance of time, we'll always share,
With whispered dreams and loving care.
In tender moments, we'll find our way,
The flame of love will never sway.

As seasons pass, the embers shine,
In the sacred space, our hearts align.
With passion's glow, we'll light the night,
An eternal flame, forever bright.

In the final dusk, when long days cease,
Our flame will burn, a lasting peace.
For love will endure, through dark and bright,
An eternal flame, a timeless light.

In the Arms of Kindness

When shadows loom and hopes are thin,
In kindness' arms, we find our kin.
With gentle words and soft embrace,
Love's tender touch, our saving grace.

Through tear-streaked nights, we hold each other,
In the warmth of care, we're sisters and brothers.
With every gesture, a healing balm,
In the chaos, a soothing calm.

With open hearts, we share our fears,
In the laughter light, we dry our tears.
Through storms we weather, hand in hand,
In kindness' glow, we understand.

With every smile, we lift the weight,
In the embrace of love, we feel fate.
Together we stand, facing the test,
In the arms of kindness, we find our rest.

As days unfold, with joy we'll see,
In every moment, a chance to be free.
In kindness' light, we'll always rise,
In this love, true strength lies.

Chapters of Togetherness

In quiet whispers, stories unfold,
Hand in hand, as days turn to gold.
Through laughter shared and tears exchanged,
We write a tale, our hearts arranged.

Each chapter rich, in dreams we weave,
With every moment, more to believe.
Together we stand, through storms and sun,
Two souls as one, our journey begun.

A memory made, in every embrace,
Time etches love, no one can replace.
Pages filled with all that we are,
Twinkling bright, like a distant star.

In the book of life, may we inscribe,
The beauty of moments that we describe.
With words unspoken and laughter true,
Together, love's written in every hue.

A Canvas of Smiles

Brushstrokes of joy, painted with care,
Colors like sunlight that dance in the air.
Each smile a stroke, so vivid, so bold,
Creating a story, a spirit to hold.

In laughter, reflections of glimmering grace,
The canvas of life, a warm, sacred space.
With hues of compassion and shades of delight,
We craft our masterpiece, shining so bright.

Every moment's a color we splatter and blend,
A tapestry woven, where hearts condescend.
As friends and as family, we gather around,
In this vibrant gallery, love knows no bound.

Through trials and triumphs, we paint and we draw,
Each smile a symbol, each frown we unthaw.
In the murals of life, together we stand,
A masterpiece formed, hand in hand.

Moments to Cherish

In fleeting seconds, memories bloom,
Captured in laughter, dispelling the gloom.
Soft whispers shared, secrets untold,
Moments to cherish, precious as gold.

Sunrise ignites, the day draws near,
In every soft glance, connection is clear.
With every heartbeat, a rhythm we find,
Through silence and chaos, our souls intertwined.

Moments like these, stitched into time,
A melody played, a sweet, silent rhyme.
In gardens of friendship, we're never alone,
Each memory thrives, in hearts it's grown.

Through sunsets of laughter, we'll walk hand in hand,
And treasure the times that life has planned.
So here's to the moments, both big and small,
In the tapestry of life, together we'll sprawl.

Sunrise of Hope

With dawn's first light, new dreams arise,
Painting the sky in vibrant dyes.
Each ray a promise, a fresh start given,
In this sunrise of hope, our spirits are driven.

Awakening dreams, like blooms in the spring,
Together, we rise and together we sing.
With shadows of doubt cast far behind,
In the warmth of the sun, our hearts are aligned.

In every heartbeat, a vision takes flight,
Holding hands, we embrace the bright light.
As the horizon glows, our fears fade away,
In this moment of grace, we choose to stay.

The world starts anew, as we stand side by side,
In the sunrise of hope, we take our stride.
With courage and faith, challenges we'll face,
In the dawn's tender glow, we find our place.

Embers of the Heart

In twilight's glow, the fire breathes,
Soft whispers float on evening's ease.
A flicker warms the chilled night air,
Love's embers dance with tender care.

Through shadowed paths, our spirits roam,
In every glance, we find a home.
With each heartbeat, the flames ignite,
A steadfast bond, our guiding light.

The world may shift, like drifting sand,
But in this warmth, we ever stand.
Together forged in passion's heat,
Our fusion makes each struggle sweet.

As seasons change, the fire grows,
In every trial, our courage shows.
Embers' glow, a promise made,
In love's embrace, we'll never fade.

With gentle hands, we stoke the fire,
For in our hearts, we build desire.
Through every storm, our spirits soar,
In the embers, we find more.

Songs of Togetherness

In harmony, our voices blend,
A melody that has no end.
Each note a step, a dance, a prayer,
In unity, we find the rare.

Through laughter shared and tears of joy,
Life's fleeting moments we employ.
With every chord, our spirits rise,
Together we're the song that flies.

In whispers soft, we tell our dreams,
The world ignites with shared themes.
Like rivers flow to oceans wide,
In songs of love, we shall abide.

When silence falls, our hearts still sing,
In quietude, sweet echoes ring.
Though trials come, we'll face them strong,
Together we compose our song.

With every breath, a verse unfolds,
In timeless rhythm, life extols.
In songs of togetherness, we'll find,
A symphony that's intertwined.

Timeless Bonds

In the garden where memories grow,
Together we plant the seeds of hope.
Through years we tend, with gentle hands,
Our timeless bonds, like ancient stands.

Through laughter bright and shadows cast,
We weave our tales, both future and past.
With every heartbeat, the ties remain,
In love's embrace, we find no pain.

As seasons change and rivers flow,
The roots run deep, the flowers glow.
Each moment shared, a thread well spun,
In this fabric, we are one.

With silver strands and wisdom's grace,
We cherish every shared embrace.
In every challenge, our spirits rise,
Timeless bonds beneath the skies.

For what is time, if not the dance,
Of souls entwined in love's sweet trance?
In every heartbeat, in every sigh,
Our timeless bonds will never die.

In the Depths of Affection

In the depths where silence sleeps,
Whispers of love flow like deep creeks.
In gentle waves, we find our ground,
Where tender feelings can abound.

Through secret paths, our hearts explore,
In every glance, we seek for more.
Together we dive into the deep,
In affection's arms, we safely keep.

With open hearts, we brave the storm,
Emerging strong, we redefine norm.
In shadows cast, our spirits shine,
For in this depth, your heart is mine.

Each moment shared, each breath we take,
Builds solid ties, unable to break.
In the ocean of love, we are free,
Navigating life, just you and me.

Through waves that rise and tides that fall,
In the depths of affection, we stand tall.
With every heartbeat, we forge our way,
Bound by the love we share each day.

The Essence of You

In the quiet depths of night,
Your laughter dances, pure delight.
A gentle breeze, a warm embrace,
In your presence, I find my place.

Memories linger, softly spun,
As daylight breaks, the new day won.
Your spirit shines, a beacon bright,
Guiding me through darkest night.

With each spoken word, you weave,
A tapestry of love to believe.
In every glance, a story unfolds,
The essence of you, a heart of gold.

Through storms and trials, side by side,
In the gentle flow, we confide.
Our dreams entwined, no need to flee,
For in your eyes, I am free.

Together we are, two hearts in one,
Creating magic with the rising sun.
In the silence, our souls unite,
The essence of you, my endless light.

Heartbeats in Harmony

Two hearts that beat in gentle rhyme,
In perfect sync, transcending time.
Each whisper shared, a lullaby,
In your gaze, I learn to fly.

Moments linger, soft and true,
As I breathe in the essence of you.
Side by side, we make our mark,
In the light, we ignite the spark.

Rhythms echo through the night,
In your arms, I find my light.
With every pulse, a promise made,
Together we will never fade.

Hand in hand, we face the storm,
In the chaos, you keep me warm.
Our hearts entwined, a sacred dance,
In harmony, we take our chance.

With every heartbeat, love will grow,
In this journey, we will flow.
Together, forever, we will stand,
Our heartbeats sing, a timeless band.

Whispered Dreams

In the twilight, dreams take flight,
Whispers soft like stars at night.
With every breath, you call my name,
Together we play this ancient game.

In shadows deep, our secrets share,
Voices linger, a tender care.
A world created just for us,
In whispered dreams, love's sacred trust.

Through the veil of sleep, we glide,
In our hearts, no need to hide.
A dance of souls, a gentle sway,
In whispered dreams, we find our way.

Bright constellations hold our fate,
In the silence, we celebrate.
Each vision sparks a vivid scene,
In whispered dreams, we reign supreme.

Awake or asleep, you're mine to keep,
In love's embrace, our feelings deep.
Together we weave the night's soft seams,
Forever bound in whispered dreams.

Portraits of Connection

A canvas stretched, a tale to tell,
Of heartbeats shared and thoughts that dwell.
In every color, a story told,
Portraits of connection, woven bold.

Strokes of laughter, hues of pain,
In the depths, we rise again.
With each embrace, a memory sown,
In the gallery of love, we've grown.

Reflections captured, light and dark,
In every shadow, we leave our mark.
Together painted, side by side,
In this masterpiece, we confide.

Brushes glide on, time stands still,
In artful silence, we find our thrill.
Connected souls, forever entwined,
In portraits of wisdom, hearts aligned.

As seasons change and colors fade,
Our bond remains, a love paraded.
In every portrait, a piece of truth,
A testament to the essence of youth.

9 789916 890974